This journal belongs to

_____

Acadia National Park

Date visited: National Park stamp:

_____

_____

_____

_____

_____

_____

_____

_____

_____

_____

_____

_____

_____

_____

Paste photo here

_____

_____

_____

_____

_____

_____

_____

_____

_____

_____

_____

_____

Arches National Park

Date visited: National Park stamp:

_____

_____

_____

_____

_____

_____

_____

_____

_____

_____

_____

_____

_____

_____

Paste photo here

_____

_____

_____

_____

_____

_____

_____

_____

_____

_____

_____

_____

_____

Badlands National Park

Date visited:

National Park stamp:

Paste photo here

_____

_____

_____

_____

_____

_____

_____

_____

_____

_____

_____

_____

Biscayne National Park

Date visited: National Park stamp:

_____

_____

_____

_____

_____

_____

_____

_____

_____

_____

_____

_____

_____

_____

Paste photo here

_____

_____

_____

_____

_____

_____

_____

_____

_____

_____

_____

_____

_____

_____

_____

Black Canyon of the Gunnison National Park

Date visited: National Park stamp:

_____

_____

_____

_____

_____

_____

_____

_____

_____

_____

_____

_____

_____

Paste photo here

Bryce Canyon National Park

Date visited: National Park stamp:

_____

_____

_____

_____

_____

_____

_____

_____

_____

_____

_____

_____

_____

_____

Paste photo here

Canyonlands National Park

Date visited: National Park stamp:

_____

_____

_____

_____

_____

_____

_____

_____

_____

_____

_____

_____

_____

_____

_____

Paste photo here

_____

_____

_____

_____

_____

_____

_____

_____

_____

_____

_____

_____

Capitol Reef National Park

Date visited: National Park stamp:

_____

_____

_____

_____

_____

_____

_____

_____

_____

_____

_____

_____

_____

_____

_____

Paste photo here

_____

_____

_____

_____

_____

_____

_____

_____

_____

_____

_____

_____

_____

Carlsbad Caverns National Park

Date visited: National Park stamp:

_____

_____

_____

_____

_____

_____

_____

_____

_____

_____

_____

_____

_____

_____

_____

Paste photo here

_____

_____

_____

_____

_____

_____

_____

_____

_____

_____

_____

_____

Channel Islands National Park

Date visited: National Park stamp:

_____

_____

_____

_____

_____

_____

_____

_____

_____

_____

_____

_____

_____

Paste photo here

_____

_____

_____

_____

_____

_____

_____

_____

_____

_____

_____

_____

_____

Congaree National Park

Date visited: National Park stamp:

Paste photo here

Crater Lake National Park

Date visited: National Park stamp:

_____

_____

_____

_____

_____

_____

_____

_____

_____

_____

_____

_____

_____

Paste photo here

Cuyahoga Valley National Park

Date visited: National Park stamp:

_____

_____

_____

_____

_____

_____

_____

_____

_____

_____

_____

_____

_____

_____

Paste photo here

_____

_____

_____

_____

_____

_____

_____

_____

_____

_____

_____

Death Valley National Park

Date visited: National Park stamp:

_____

_____

_____

_____

_____

_____

_____

_____

_____

_____

_____

_____

_____

Paste photo here

_____

_____

_____

_____

_____

_____

_____

_____

_____

_____

_____

_____

Denali National Park

Date visited: National Park stamp:

_____

_____

_____

_____

_____

_____

_____

_____

_____

_____

_____

_____

_____

_____

Paste photo here

_____

_____

_____

_____

_____

_____

_____

_____

_____

_____

_____

_____

_____

Dry Tortugas National Park

Date visited: National Park stamp:

_____

_____

_____

_____

_____

_____

_____

_____

_____

_____

_____

_____

_____

_____

Paste photo here

_____

_____

_____

_____

_____

_____

_____

_____

_____

_____

_____

Everglades National Park

Date visited: National Park stamp:

_____

_____

_____

_____

_____

_____

_____

_____

_____

_____

_____

_____

_____

_____

Paste photo here

Gates of the Arctic National Park

Date visited: National Park stamp:

_____

_____

_____

_____

_____

_____

_____

_____

_____

_____

_____

_____

_____

_____

Paste photo here

Gateway Arch National Park

Date visited: National Park stamp:

_____

_____

_____

_____

_____

_____

_____

_____

_____

_____

_____

_____

_____

_____

Paste photo here

Glacier Bay National Park

Date visited: National Park stamp:

Paste photo here

Glacier National Park

Date visited: National Park stamp:

_____

_____

_____

_____

_____

_____

_____

_____

_____

_____

_____

_____

_____

_____

_____

Paste photo here

Grand Canyon National Park

Date visited: National Park stamp:

_____

_____

_____

_____

_____

_____

_____

_____

_____

_____

_____

_____

_____

Paste photo here

Grand Teton National Park

Date visited:

National Park stamp:

Grand Teton National Park
MAY 3 1 2022
Moose, Wyoming

Paste photo here

Great Basin National Park

Date visited: National Park stamp:

_____

_____

_____

_____

_____

_____

_____

_____

_____

_____

_____

_____

_____

_____

Paste photo here

Great Sand Dunes National Park

Date visited: National Park stamp:

_____

_____

_____

_____

_____

_____

_____

_____

_____

_____

_____

_____

_____

_____

Paste photo here

Great Smoky Mountains National Park

Date visited: National Park stamp:

_____

_____

_____

_____

_____

_____

_____

_____

_____

_____

_____

_____

_____

_____

_____

Paste photo here

Guadalupe National Park

Date visited: National Park stamp:

_____

_____

_____

_____

_____

_____

_____

_____

_____

_____

_____

_____

_____

_____

Paste photo here

_____

_____

_____

_____

_____

_____

_____

_____

_____

_____

_____

_____

_____

Haleakala National Park

Date visited: National Park stamp:

_____

_____

_____

_____

_____

_____

_____

_____

_____

_____

_____

_____

_____

Paste photo here

Hawai'i Volcanoes National Park

Date visited:

National Park stamp:

_____

_____

_____

_____

_____

_____

_____

_____

_____

_____

_____

_____

_____

_____

Paste photo here

_____

_____

_____

_____

_____

_____

_____

_____

_____

_____

_____

_____

Hot Springs National Park

Date visited: National Park stamp:

_____

_____

_____

_____

_____

_____

_____

_____

_____

_____

_____

_____

_____

_____

Paste photo here

_____

_____

_____

_____

_____

_____

_____

_____

_____

_____

_____

_____

Indiana Dunes National Park

Date visited: National Park stamp:

Paste photo here

Isle Royale National Park

Date visited: National Park stamp:

_____

_____

_____

_____

_____

_____

_____

_____

_____

_____

_____

_____

_____

_____

Paste photo here

Joshua Tree National Park

Date visited: National Park stamp:

_____

_____

_____

_____

_____

_____

_____

_____

_____

_____

_____

_____

_____

_____

Paste photo here

_____

_____

_____

_____

_____

_____

_____

_____

_____

_____

_____

_____

Katmai National Park

Date visited: National Park stamp:

_____

_____

_____

_____

_____

_____

_____

_____

_____

_____

_____

_____

_____

Paste photo here

_____

_____

_____

_____

_____

_____

_____

_____

_____

_____

_____

_____

Kenai Fjords National Park

Date visited: National Park stamp:

_____

_____

_____

_____

_____

_____

_____

_____

_____

_____

_____

_____

_____

_____

Paste photo here

Kings Canyon National Park

Date visited: National Park stamp:

_____

_____

_____

_____

_____

_____

_____

_____

_____

_____

_____

_____

_____

_____

Paste photo here

Kobuk Valley National Park

Date visited: National Park stamp:

_____

_____

_____

_____

_____

_____

_____

_____

_____

_____

_____

_____

_____

_____

Paste photo here

Lake Clark National Park

Date visited: National Park stamp:

_____

_____

_____

_____

_____

_____

_____

_____

_____

_____

_____

_____

_____

_____

Paste photo here

Lassen Volcanic National Park

Date visited: National Park stamp:

_____

_____

_____

_____

_____

_____

_____

_____

_____

_____

_____

_____

_____

_____

_____

_____

Paste photo here

_____

_____

_____

_____

_____

_____

_____

_____

_____

_____

_____

_____

_____

Mammoth Cave National Park

Date visited: National Park stamp:

_____

_____

_____

_____

_____

_____

_____

_____

_____

_____

_____

_____

_____

Paste photo here

_____

_____

_____

_____

_____

_____

_____

_____

_____

_____

_____

_____

_____

Mesa Verde National Park

Date visited: National Park stamp:

_____

_____

_____

_____

_____

_____

_____

_____

_____

_____

_____

_____

_____

_____

Paste photo here

Mount Rainier National Park

Date visited: National Park stamp:

_____

_____

_____

_____

_____

_____

_____

_____

_____

_____

_____

_____

_____

_____

Paste photo here

National Park of American Samoa

Date visited: National Park stamp:

_____

_____

_____

_____

_____

_____

_____

_____

_____

_____

_____

_____

_____

_____

_____

Paste photo here

_____

_____

_____

_____

_____

_____

_____

_____

_____

_____

_____

_____

_____

New River Gorge National Park

Date visited: National Park stamp:

_____

_____

_____

_____

_____

_____

_____

_____

_____

_____

_____

_____

_____

_____

Paste photo here

North Cascades National Park

Date visited: National Park stamp:

_____

_____

_____

_____

_____

_____

_____

_____

_____

_____

_____

_____

_____

_____

Paste photo here

Olympic National Park

Date visited: National Park stamp:

_____

_____

_____

_____

_____

_____

_____

_____

_____

_____

_____

_____

_____

_____

_____

Paste photo here

Petrified Forest National Park

Date visited: National Park stamp:

_____

_____

_____

_____

_____

_____

_____

_____

_____

_____

_____

_____

_____

_____

_____

Paste photo here

Pinnacles National Park

Date visited: National Park stamp:

_____

_____

_____

_____

_____

_____

_____

_____

_____

_____

_____

_____

_____

Paste photo here

_____

_____

_____

_____

_____

_____

_____

_____

_____

_____

_____

Redwood National National Park

Date visited: National Park stamp:

_____

_____

_____

_____

_____

_____

_____

_____

_____

_____

_____

_____

_____

Paste photo here

Rocky Mountain National Park

Date visited: National Park stamp:

_____

_____

_____

_____

_____

_____

_____

_____

_____

_____

_____

_____

_____

_____

_____

Paste photo here

Saguaro National Park

Date visited: National Park stamp:

_____

_____

_____

_____

_____

_____

_____

_____

_____

_____

_____

_____

_____

_____

Paste photo here

_____

_____

_____

_____

_____

_____

_____

_____

_____

_____

_____

_____

_____

Sequoia National Park

Date visited: National Park stamp:

_____

_____

_____

_____

_____

_____

_____

_____

_____

_____

_____

_____

_____

_____

Paste photo here

_____

_____

_____

_____

_____

_____

_____

_____

_____

_____

_____

_____

_____

Shenandoah National Park

Date visited: National Park stamp:

_____

_____

_____

_____

_____

_____

_____

_____

_____

_____

_____

_____

_____

_____

_____

Paste photo here

Theodore Roosevelt National Park

Date visited: National Park stamp:

_____

_____

_____

_____

_____

_____

_____

_____

_____

_____

_____

_____

_____

_____

Paste photo here

_____

_____

_____

_____

_____

_____

_____

_____

_____

_____

_____

_____

Virgin Islands National Park

Date visited: National Park stamp:

_____

_____

_____

_____

_____

_____

_____

_____

_____

_____

_____

_____

_____

_____

Paste photo here

_____

_____

_____

_____

_____

_____

_____

_____

_____

_____

_____

_____

_____

Voyageurs National Park

Date visited: National Park stamp:

_____

_____

_____

_____

_____

_____

_____

_____

_____

_____

_____

_____

_____

_____

Paste photo here

_____

_____

_____

_____

_____

_____

_____

_____

_____

_____

_____

_____

White Sands National Park

Date visited: National Park stamp:

_____

_____

_____

_____

_____

_____

_____

_____

_____

_____

_____

_____

_____

_____

_____

Paste photo here

Wind Cave National Park

Date visited: National Park stamp:

_____

_____

_____

_____

_____

_____

_____

_____

_____

_____

_____

_____

_____

Paste photo here

Wrangell-St. Elias National Park

Date visited: National Park stamp:

_____

_____

_____

_____

_____

_____

_____

_____

_____

_____

_____

_____

_____

_____

_____

Paste photo here

Yellowstone National Park

Date visited:

National Park stamp:

JUN 03 2022

Yellowstone National Park
Visitor Center

Paste photo here

_____

_____

_____

_____

_____

_____

_____

_____

_____

_____

_____

_____

_____

Yosemite National Park

Date visited: National Park stamp:

_____

_____

_____

_____

_____

_____

_____

_____

_____

_____

_____

_____

_____

_____

Paste photo here

_____

_____

_____

_____

_____

_____

_____

_____

_____

_____

_____

Zion National Park

Date visited: National Park stamp:

_____

_____

_____

_____

_____

_____

_____

_____

_____

_____

_____

_____

_____

_____

Paste photo here

My hikes

Name:

Distance:

Date hiked:

Name:

Distance:

Date hiked:

Name:

Distance:

Date hiked:

Name:

Distance:

Date hiked:

Name:

Distance:

Date hiked:

Name:

Distance:

Date hiked:

Name:

Distance:

Date hiked:

Name:

Distance:

Date hiked:

Name:

Distance:

Date hiked:

Name:

Distance:

Date hiked:

Name:

Distance:

Date hiked:

Name:

Distance:

Date hiked:

Name:

Distance:

Date hiked:

Name:

Distance:

Date hiked:

Name:

Distance:

Date hiked:

Name:

Distance:

Date hiked:

Name:

Distance:

Date hiked:

Name:

Distance:

Date hiked:

Name:

Distance:

Date hiked:

Name:

Distance:

Date hiked:

Notes

Prompts

1. What made you decide to visit this national park in the first place?

2. What blew your mind the most about that national park?

3. What sights would you recommend that friends and family visit?

4. Did you see any wildlife? What kind?

5. Did you try any of the local foods or restaurants?

6. How did you feel when you first arrived?

7. Did you go for a hike? What did you see?

8. How did this national park compare to any of the others you've been to?

Fort Laramie National Historic Site
MAY 28 2022
Fort Laramie, WY

Little Bighorn Ba...
JUN 09
Crow Agency...

Little Bighorn Battlefield NM
JUN 09 2022
Crow Agency, MT

JUN 10 2022
Devils Tower National Monument

National Monument
JUN 10 2022
Devils Tower, WY

Made in the USA
Monee, IL
17 December 2021